Dead Man walking

Death from Within

By: Deborah Lynn

Acknowledgments

First and foremost, I dedicate this book to my Lord and Savior Jesus' Christ, the ruler and super ruler of my life. If it had not been for the Lord this book wouldn't have been written. He guided me to write so that others going through trails may be healed, delivered and set free. Although each person's situation is different, God never changes. It was His constant *Love* that kept me going through the journey that was set before me. Also, his tender *Mercy* held me when I couldn't keep myself. I'm forever in his debt for all he's done for me besides, I trust him with every fiber of my being. His Spirit envelops my heart in a gentle, loving way. Thank you, JESUS for breathing the breath of life on my being and never letting me go!

Dedication

I dedicate this book to anyone that can't seem to find freedom. But, most of all I dedicate this book to the only true and living God of Abraham, Isaac, and Jacob who created me to press through no matter the cost. Also, keep in mind that my story is *my story* and each person's story is always different from another. What am I saying? Just because God allowed me to go this route, it doesn't mean someone else will go through trails the same way. But, press in; press through and never, ever give up!

Table of Contents

Instructions

It was November 1, 2016. I was given instructions by God. He spoke to me in the night while I was asleep. He told me I would write a book. The title would be, *"Dead Man Walking"* with a subtitle, *"Death from Within."*

Secondly, my instructions were to "call the hospital to interview a doctor on this matter." Only one physician returned my call and replied, "I'll do it." Everyone else I asked replied, "It's the holiday, many are on vacation and others are too busy at the hospital." Oh, but not Dr. Karen Looman, D.O. It wasn't the fact that she had time, she made time for me even though her time was limited. I am thankful from the bottom of my heart for her kindness! May the blessings of the Lord be upon you always, Dr. Looman, D.O.

My next instruction was to write about the human body's smell of death. The paradox *was that I didn't realized at the time that I had already died within my own being "Death from Within.*

My Story

The attacks came at me in all forms, even a snake bite while in a dream on my jaw. I took the snake by the head and threw it away from me shouting, "Jesus!" You must know, this was something I've never encountered before and hope to never experience again. I was also bitten by a yellow cat, attacked by a white cat and terrified by a black cat. All of these experiences came to me while asleep. Please understand that the devil is wicked and does most of his evil in the midnight hour. These experiences allowed me to know that witchcraft was coming against me. In one dream there was a black spider hanging over my head for who knows how long. As time went on God showed me that the spider had no more legs to stand on. Later in a dream He showed me the spider; it only had half of a head left. Finally, it was dead and disappeared. There was still more that needed to be dealt with and much more to share. Continue to read on, please.

Yes, I know my dreams are a hard pill to swallow but this is real and true. Besides, it's part of my life's story. God told me to write my story. Out of obedience I'm writing my story for someone to read for whatever reason.

Not really understanding myself nor the depth that it entails but, Almighty God, through the Holy Spirit within me has been my coach to guide me in writing this book to help whomever I can. Hopefully someone will be able to relate to my story and gain clarity in understanding of his/her situation for victory.

I'm still trying to get the gist of what happened in this season of my life. Therefore, Holy Spirit, I invite you to come on this roller-coaster ride with me as I attempt to write this book for whomever needs to read it. Take over my hand as the truth is being unveiled. *My heart is welling forth [with] a good matter: I say what I have composed touching the King. My tongue is the pen of a ready writer." Psalms 45:1 (Darby Bible)*

These stories came from different sources, people and my own situations, namely:

- Ex-Husbands

- Generational Curses

- Myself

- Pastors

- Word Curses

I'm still in training and I am learning to use the resources God has provided through His Word as well as the teachings I received from the following deliverance ministries:

Open Heaven Ministries, Wings of Refuge (Louisville, KY), Roots and Branches, along with Zion's Fire Revival Ministries who played a BIG part in some of my healings and deliverance (*Used by permission*). ***"For the weapons of our warfare are not carnal, but mighty through God to the pulling down of strongholds." 2 Corinthians 10:4 (KJV)***

This battle solely had to be dealt with in the realm of the spirit. Why? Because these events that happened to me were spiritual matters that I needed to experience for the benefit of others who need deliverance.

Powerpoint Church

In 1998, I joined Powerpoint Church and remained there for four years of revelation, knowledge and teachings.

Out of all of the churches I've attended, this church was the most powerful, anointed, revelatory church I've ever been a part of. Bishop Roll would come in ready for service and it was obvious he studied the word of God and loved it. We couldn't wait to get to church on Tuesdays and Sundays! Bishop Roll was so faithful in the word of God that he never, ever talked about himself. I wondered why he never shared his testimony with us. Maybe he'd already shared with the congregation years back; I never asked. He was doing what he was called to do and that was to preach the word of God in season with power!

God told Bishop Roll who was to get licensed for ministry and that's what happened. He didn't waste any time doing it. On Friday nights he let us know who was going to speak; that was our training ground.

At this high time of anointing when I would go to work, two pastors that worked in my department would pull up a chair and say, "talk." And, I'd say, "get it started."

Revelation would just flow out of my mouth, but to me, I was just sharing. They told me that I didn't realize what was in me. While sitting there, listening to me it seemed as though they looked like two hungry birds being fed and they enjoyed every bit of it! Sometimes Donna, my co-worker, would come over to our group on break and turn around to leave. She understood that the Lord was working with the two ministers and me.

There were three females that lived in Ohio (two of them were named Jill and Melinda). They would come on Sundays and once a month for our women's ministry. All three of them were anointed and well-groomed by Bishop and Pastor Roll for years. They were spiritual daughters; groomed and trained before I ever arrived.

The body of Christ was so full of revelation sometimes we'd be overwhelmed and had to go home and lay down; at least that's what was happening with me.

In service, Pastor Roll, Bishop's wife, would lay on the steps in the sanctuary when the anointing would come in so strong. She always got up with something to share. Not just her, but other congregants as well. The body of Christ at Powerpoint was so anointed yet our attitudes and behaviors were out of order. There were two female members of the congregation that were over the finances who had strict control as well. There was discord in the body, backbiting, division, gossip even between two female pastors even though I had only seen it once but not with the Bishop. We had yard sales to make money for the church. I know, I know! If everyone gave their tithes back to God we wouldn't have to sell, but we did, and we enjoyed doing it all at the same time. However, it was no problem for me to give my tithes to God because my mother taught our family to tithe when we got our first jobs and I never stopped, praise God!

During service one day Bishop Roll was preaching and all of a sudden, he started saying things that made us all start to laugh so hard on one accord. On the floor laughing I went. We were screaming and laughing from our guts. That had never happened before. When we were finished laughing, Bishop Roll said, "Keep it that way" (on one accord)! Then, he began to preach again. But occasionally we continued to laugh, but Bishop Roll just smiled and kept preaching.

In 2007, God told me it was time to leave. I'd been praying about this as well. I was on my way to Bible Study. When I arrived the two female pastors were already there. I shared with them what God told me. The perplexed look on their faces showed me how dumbfounded they were. I returned the door key and went on my way.

As I shut the door behind me, while going to my car, I literally heard chains fall off my ankles. What a relief to walk away in freedom! I'll explain more later…

Now, what I am about to share here is a very serious matter that changed the lives of the people at Powerpoint Church in a very negative, ugly way. Please know and believe that I'm sharing this bit of information with you to make you aware that some leaders need help just as anyone else. They are human beings; not God. That's why it's so important that we keep our eyes focused on the Lord Jesus who is the head of the church. Disappointments will come but realize this: ***"It is better to take refuge in the Lord than to trust in people." Psalms 118:8 (NLT)***

About one year after I'd left Powerpoint Church, Pastor Roll called me. She hadn't returned any of my phone calls before and I had stopped trying to contact her. She called and apologized to me for everything that happened in the past. I accepted her apology. She began to share with me what happened. She thought I knew, but I didn't. I hadn't talked to anyone there after leaving. I had no idea what she was getting ready to share. Six months prior to my leaving, Jill from Ohio, told me she was mad because I'd left too soon but I never knew. Pastor Roll shared that Bishop Roll, her husband, began having an affair with Melinda from Ohio, who was one of his spiritual daughters. People were calling Pastor Roll telling her that Bishop Roll and Melinda were parked at the church all hours of the night on weekends. She shared with me that Bishop Roll had left home. I screamed at this news! Again, she thought I knew, but no! Pastor Roll shared that she hemmed Melinda up in the basement of the church because she had known what was going on. Melinda ended up leaving the church and Bishop Roll moved to the upstairs area of the church to live. My heart jumped so fast that it scared me.

Melinda became pregnant. Bishop Roll divorced Pastor Roll and married Melinda, who was about 30 years younger. All I could do was apologize to Pastor Roll for what she had endured. Pastor Roll didn't tell me this but one of the young ladies from Ohio told me that Pastor Roll had also suffered a stroke. She denied it in the beginning, but later told me that it was true.

I asked Pastor Roll, "Is there anything else?" She told me, "That's about it." All of this information had burdened my heart so that in my prayer time to God I prayed, "Lord, heal Pastor Roll's heart. Help her to forgive her husband and the young lady. I'm sure she's bitter in her heart. Help her Lord and cleanse her with your precious blood, in Jesus' name." I guess the worst thing about this whole fiasco is that this young lady was their spiritual daughter who they had groomed and reared from her youth! Wow! Sharing this story hurt me, but it's true no matter how painful it is to even write. Bishop Roll and Melinda are still married to this day. Lord, I pray that all leaders turn their hearts to you first and foremost. Bishop Roll is really sick now. My prayers go out to him.

Gathering Church

It was about 2001 when I joined Gathering Church which was a very prophetic and anointed church in which Prophet Port was the overseer. We moved so many times from one place after another. It was the most unstable fellowship I'd ever encountered in my church life.

One year we moved downtown and rented a floor upstairs in a high-rise hotel that was empty. It was a telephone company on that particular floor at one time and it was very creepy and eerie. There were all kinds of spirits lingering in the halls. There were many rooms on that floor, but we only occupied a few.

My stomach would continuously hurt something terrible in the services as if I were in labor. I would hold my stomach and Prophet Port would see me but, he never said anything. One day I told Prophet Port about a dream that God showed me. The dream meant that it was time for me to preach the gospel. Prophet Port begin to mentor me but only a couple of times. He really was to thrust me forward through discipling me just as he did some of the other leaders, but he didn't. It appeared that he was ignoring my dream to preach. Prophet Port kept me at a standstill because he would not fully pour into me. At one point he said, "I'm not casting my pearls before swine," indicating that he felt many weren't worthy of his time which included me! Prophet Port even allowed every other leader to speak but he ignored me even when a few of the other leader's spoke up for me. Eventually I felt there was no room for me at Gathering Church. God told Prophet Port I was leaving the church and that's exactly what I did.

This is the story of my marriage to Billy: I had been attending Gathering Church for five years at this point and a young man joined the church whose name was Billy. After several months Billy approached me and ask me out on a date to the theatre. Initially, I declined. The following week he asked me, but I told him, I was fasting. I was so focused on God that I simply wasn't interested in Billy's request. Eventually, after a third request I consented. During one service after we had dated a few months Prophet Port was preaching to the body of Christ at large. He begins to prophesy. At one point he said to me from the pulpit, "Deborah, I know who your husband is," and just after that he said "Billy, I know who your wife is." After we'd heard the word from Prophet Port, Billy and I shared that we'd hoped it was each other. We dated for a year and got married at the courthouse. He left his apartment to move in with me in my condo and the next few years were a roller-coaster ride.

It was less than a year of being married when strange things began to happen with Billy. In the midnight hour while asleep, he would begin to make strange sounds and move about in the bed as if something was attacking him. These attacks became increasingly worst over a period of months. He would be saying things like, "I rebuke you Satan in the name of Jesus!" Most times I would put my hand on him, not knowing what was going on, but hollering out, "Jesus" to cast off whatever was on him. Then, we would go back to sleep. The following morning, I asked him, "What happened?" He'd say, "Something was attacking me on my body." "How long has this been going on?" I'd ask. He would say something like 'for a while now.' But I knew in my spirit it had been happening before our marriage. Yet, he never got any help. Sometimes, he'd tell me what happened and sometimes he wouldn't say anything. Yet, I always prayed with concern and didn't know who to consult about the matter. Billy never gave me a heads up before we got married. I always felt it was wrong of him not to tell me of this situation. I felt so helpless. Had I known this concerning him I would've run for my life in the opposite direction as if hell fire was under my feet, to say the least!

So, there I was, in a situation I've never experienced before. As time went on, the same thing continued over and over until one day I went to our pastor to tell the whole story. Billy had never mentioned this to anyone. It was necessary for us to get help because this demonic activity had to go, and it wasn't going to go on its own!

On March 20, 2011, I had a dream that was a key to our predicament. In the dream, Billy and I was somewhere, and he pulled something out of his bag. To me it looked like a big thick square pencil. But, when I got up close, it looked like a long bottle of clear liquid with a name on it. I couldn't read the name that was on it. Billy said, "Who put this in my bag?" I said, "I did, while second guessing myself." Billy said, "No you didn't! I know who did." "Who did this?" I asked. Then, a guy walked up to Billy and told him who put the bottle in his bag, but Billy wouldn't tell me. It was revealed to me in the dream that the stick represented evil (witchcraft). The next morning, I shared the dream with Billy asking him if he knew what it meant. But he nonchalantly said, "No." Again, I sought Prophet Port for help, but he said, "Billy never said anything to him." By this time, I realized that I had to get us some help because it wasn't going to happen with Prophet Port. Besides, I didn't know if he could handle the matter and I wasn't going to wait around and see. Our lives were in jeopardy. Prophet Port was disappointed because Billy wouldn't share anything with him even though Billy was his armor-bearer. Imagine that!

After that experience, I realized that demons are as real as Jesus dying on the cross. I too began to experience demonic attacks in the same way as Billy. I remember Prophet Port telling Billy, "Deborah never dealt with anything like this before you two got married." Prophet Port was my pastor for many years, and he knew me well. When the demonic attacks came upon me, I'd said, "What the….is this? How dare you touch my body! I plead the blood of Jesus over myself in the name of Jesus! You filthy, nasty demon! I place you under my feet in Jesus' name! The blood of Jesus is against you!" I went off the deep end! When things began to happen to me it was a whole new ball game! There was no more wasted time here. We needed help ASAP!

As time moved on, I started having stomach pains again as if I were in labor. I'd ask the Lord what this was, but I never received an answer whatsoever. We began to go to the emergency room to see if there was something physically wrong with me and if they could tell me anything. My visits were to no avail, nothing. Even though in my spirit, I knew it was a spiritual matter. The pain lasted from 2011-2018.

I didn't just experience stomach pains, but I was having ungodly demonic attacks during worship service. When worship would get to a high peak with everyone praising God, I would begin to hear weird sounds during worship. The enemy would interfere during my time of worship. If you were close enough to me, you could hear the enemy making these ungodly sounds. I'd shout "Jesus! The blood of Jesus!" One day, one of the mothers of the church came over to me, grabbed my hand and ran me around the church about five (5) times. I wanted to die from embarrassment. I was told by the mother of the church that my husband sat there crying as this was happening. That was a bit of a surprise because it wasn't something that has happened before. I went to speak to Prophet Port in his office after the service, he said to me, "You should've seen your face." But he gave me no advice on anything in order to help me. That's the part I never understood and still don't except that maybe, just maybe he didn't know what to do.

In prayer, while seeking the Lord, my question to Him was, "What door has been left open for the enemy to come in?" Is it un-forgiveness, anger, bitterness, what Lord? I never received a response. That's when I began to seek deliverance. I didn't know anything or anyone that could help me. I would ask God to put people before me that would be able to properly walk me through this matter. He revealed to me deliverance ministries. I continued to experience the same thing, but no one knew how to help. Then, finally Prophet Port gave me advice to go see Minister Mabel. She was an anointed vessel in the area of deliverance. She had spoken at our church on several occasions as well. That gave me somewhat of a relief. Layers of issues from my youth were being removed. Yet, there was still something lingering that I couldn't put my finger on. All I knew was that God told me someone was working witchcraft and that's it. That's when I received personal deliverance, one on one with Minister Mabel.

My husband kept most of what he went through to himself and hide what he wouldn't share with me. In other words, a lot was covered up that I knew not of, sad to say. But this event couldn't be hidden because what I'm about to share was happening with Billy and then it began to happen to me as well. I told Minister Mabel what had been happening in the mid night hour that a lust spirit would attack certain parts of his body. Later, the same thing happened to me and that's why I came for help. It was too much for me to handle and I needed some reinforcements.

Minister Mabel explained that these spirits are called, "Incubus and Succubus." As a married couple, the two become one, yes. Incubus spirits seek to have encounters with sleeping women in their dreams. Succubus spirits seek to have sexual encounters with men in their dreams all the same. This is what we went through, but my husband wouldn't go see Minister Mabel at this point. That's why I had to do it alone, so I ran to see her. I'd suggest you research this for more information on "Incubus and Succubus spirits."

Minister Mabel took the time to explain this to me. She had me buy a book on this matter that she sold in her Christian Book Store, where she had spiritual warfare books. I'd go to her and she would minister to me and eventually my husband did join on one occasion. But, after that he didn't seek any more help. Minister Mabel instructed us to fast for seven days while praying the prayers from the book. To be honest, I don't remember the name of the book and she no longer has the bookstore. We did what she told us to do and that was the end of that, praise God! I thank God for all deliverance ministries for the Kingdom of God.

I was still experiencing other demonic attacks but much, much less than before. I would pray often, ***"I do believe, Lord; help my little faith!" Mark 9:24b (The Passion Translation).*** As time went on, I found out my husband was seeing someone other than myself. This started when he went to his reunion party and exchanged numbers with an old high school classmate. He never asked me to go to the reunion with him. Besides, I didn't really want to go anyway. There was a change in him shortly thereafter with me. He began to sleep in the TV room a lot more than the norm. He also didn't want to perform. I felt rejected by my husband and began to go to more deliverance classes as well as seek God even the more. I was in despair to say the least. Although I was attending these classes, I began to spend more time by myself and go to bed much earlier than the norm. He'd gotten a second job at night but wouldn't let me know where he was working. I wondered; now why did he do that?

After a while, the Lord told me to return back to Gathering Church because at the time, my husband was still there. I returned out of obedience. Around 2011 my husband left the church because he was involved in his own sin and didn't want to be exposed. All the while, he deceived me. Not long after, I left the church again, but was still dealing with stomach pains. I had to stay strong and not give up. The stomach pains kept coming and I just kept going into warfare; rebuking the spirit of witchcraft and casting it out in Jesus' name. I was so confused and couldn't get any answers. I will speak on this more later. But the pains would go on for about 10-15 minutes. I spoke breakthrough in Jesus' name and declared that I was going to walk in what God had purposed for me no matter the cost.

One night my husband left to go to his second job. It was a dark and rainy evening and he can't see that well in the dark. I wanted to find out where he worked or spending all his time at night, so I followed him. He first went to our storage unit to place something in it. As I continued to follow him, he went to a bank, got out of the car and went to unlock the bank's door. I said to myself, "Okay, he really does have a second job." As he put the key in to unlock the door a female opened the door from the inside and they kissed! Yes! That's what I said, they kissed! He proceeded to go inside. Can you imagine? She must have finished cleaning at the bank because he threw out the trash. They left there and I continued to follow him to a second business to clean as well. This is how I found out he was seeing someone other than myself. It wasn't a good feeling but, the matter had to be dealt with somehow. What was I going to do concerning the matter? Should I kill him? Poison him? This is where the enemy comes in like a flood to get you to do something crazy. No! I decided we were going to sit down like two normal human beings. Instead of going off the deep end I would deal with this in a reasonable manner and blow his mind. I thought, "It's God's way."

When he finally got home that early morning, I didn't say a word. Arguing was not the solution to the matter and I refused to go there. It gave me time to think. When I arrived at work, I called him and said, "Don't you get paid this Friday?" He said, "Yes, why?" Because, when you get paid, I want you to move out and the locks will be changed as well." Billy said, "Why?" I told him I saw him at the bank when he kissed his co-worker as if she was his wife and he had been deceiving me just as I sensed. I also told him that he had to move out before I got home. And, that's exactly what Billy did, leave. When I arrived home, I felt a relief in my spirit. It was time for me to do some spring cleaning. Everything he left had to go so, I took what he left to his mother's house which was not far from where I lived. Over the next few months everything that he sat or laid on had to go! I cleaned and prayed throughout my home we shared; anointing the windows, doors, rooms, doorknobs, vents, plugs, computers, phone, TV; to say the least! I anointed everything possible. And, threw out the bed, mattress, pillowcases, pillows, sheets and anything else I felt the need to get rid of in order to begin a new start. Even Billy's mail couldn't come in the house. It's called house cleansing.

A week went by, I came home, and their Billy was, with his feet propped up as he was washing his clothes and relaxing. His keys were on the table and I picked up the keys and told Billy, "This is your last time coming here!" He hurried up and packed his clothes and left. What in the world was he thinking? That it's okay? NO! I had his keys and wanted to make sure he didn't make a second set. Still dealing with what was oppressing me, I didn't need any extra mess lingering around. After all, the attacks were enough, and they were still occurring. A married man of God is supposed to protect the wife and children as well as provide for them. What's the difference between a man of God not following the guidelines of the word and an unsaved man? There is no difference. ***"But I would have you know, that the head of every man is Christ; and the head of the woman is the man; and the head of Christ is God." I Corinthians 11:3 (KJV).***

I am not really sure if a female had anything to do with what he brought into our home. I wish he would have told me what was going on before we got married. That's how I found out there's help for everything. You have to seek out what you need. Had I known before we got married, to tell the truth, I wouldn't have married him. It's the honorable, respectful way of doing the right thing with integrity. Read ***Psalms 55:1-23.*** This is concerning betrayal.

My total dependency was on the Lord who had my undivided attention. My prayer life increased because God was my everything! I lived and breathed Him. He was my dependency for life, period. Yet, my mind was in turmoil wondering what in the world could I've done to deserve this punishment. All of those years having read about the devil and his imps was one thing but to have experienced it was another.

The stomach pains started again one early morning around 3:00 AM so I went back to the emergency room at the nearest hospital. They did an ultrasound and found two small gall stones in my side. They didn't think that was the cause of the pain. I was sent home again. This went on for 6 years (2012-2017). My physician would tell me to go to the emergency room, but no; I would just go home. Every now and then, I'd experience this stomach pain and I'd continue to rebuke the pain in Jesus' name, but nothing seemed to work. I was determined to get to the bottom of this matter. I went back to my doctor and asked him to send me to a specialist for the pain and to do something different. He gave me a referral back to the hospital for a sonogram this time. Guess what? It was the gall stones after all; they had enlarged. I was set up for emergency surgery. My gall bladder was removed in January 2018 and I felt like a brand-new woman! All of those years of pain and misdiagnosis. My struggle in the midnight hour was over as far as the stomach pains were concerned. Yet, I was still dealing with some demonic attacks but without pain.

Fear crept in my life at this point, so I dreaded going to sleep. A couple days per week I would get attacked by the evil one and would take authority by saying, "I plead the blood of Jesus!" as loud as I could. I would command the witchcraft spirit to go! Whatever came out of my spirit was spoken. I was knowledgeable about the authority that I had been given through the word of God. So, I pleaded the blood of Jesus because the power is in the Name. *Luke 10:19 (KJV)* **states:** *"Behold, I give you power to tread upon serpents and scorpions, and over all the power of the enemy: and nothing shall by any means hurt you."*

Finally, when I would get into a deep sleep: I'd be awakened by animal sounds such as a snake hissing in my bedroom which would cause me to raise my head up so fast you would've thought it was real. In the spirit realm it was real. The enemy will come in any way to cause fear and torment, but one must keep using the word of God. That's why studying to show yourselves approved unto God is so important. In time of need the word of God will give peace and steadfastness instead of panicking and fear. I would say, "I take authority over witchcraft spirit in the name of Jesus! Go!" Then, I'd get out of the bed no matter the time and anoint my bed and anything else I felt led to anoint.

Then, I'd go back to bed and ask God for sweet sleep and that's what happened, especially when I was tired. Fear was fierce for a long time. So, I continued getting help by attending deliverance ministries because I wasn't hearing anything from God at that time in my life. In spite of what was going on, I knew I had to keep moving. I remembered reading what Whitney Houston would tell her daughter to do. She would tell her daughter, "Keep moving baby." Therefore, I did what she told her daughter to do.

Next, as I began to look around in my home, I'd ask God, "Is there anything here that needs to go? Please allow me to know so it can be removed." One-night God showed me a colorful bracelet. As soon as day broke, I jumped out of my bed, but not fast enough, to put the bracelet in a brown paper bag. I took that bag and my hammer to the dumpster and beat the hell out of it! Then, threw it in the dumpster. I said to God, "Anything else?" That was all at the time, but that didn't fix what was still lingering in my home. Yet, little by little it seems as though the attacks were getting less and less.

As time went on, I continued to dread going to bed at night because at different times, the attacks would come against my mind. I never, ever thought such a thing would happen to me. I needed help desperately. There were times when I was exhausted, but I wasn't going to surrender to the enemy's tactics. Never, ever allow anyone to speak words of death in your spiritual ear gate. Cancel every negative word that comes into your spirit. Tell them, "I don't receive any negativity," even if it's your mama saying the wrong thing.

Each day that I awakened I felt a bit of a release just starting over again. I would do my morning devotion and that would start my day. "Lord," I would say, "Is there anyone else in the world going through anything similar to what I'm going through?" All I knew to do was to study concerning the attacks of the evil one and get help from ministries that dealt with this level of deliverance. Thank God for ministries that are equipped to help deliver souls from torment.

I'd like to share with you concerning *unforgiveness* in your heart. I learned from a class on unforgiveness that refusing to forgive can cause you to be hindered in moving forward. We all need to be free from hindrances in our lives period. Even when it's hard to forgive at times, it's necessary for you to be free. Unforgiveness will take a toll on your spirit, soul and body; you won't even realize the damage it does to your blood pressure, heart, and thoughts. Forgive others and yourself. In that way the enemy won't have that hold on you: free yourself! Whom the Son sets free is free indeed! When I started forgiving all those people in my past life, and even now, all kinds of shackles began to fall off me. You must know that the older you are the more issues you have unless you've repented and forgiven those that caused you pain. They're not worth you being hindered. Now, it's easy for me to forgive anyone as well as bless them now, praise God! But it does take time when in fact it took me years to be honest. We were created to forgive. Just do it! It's a release from within you. Because of that, layers came off my life of hindrances. Oh, taste and see that the Lord is good! Please pray with me now.

Prayer: Father, I come to you in Jesus' name. Forgive me for having unforgiveness in my heart. I now know who the battle is with. The thief that comes to steal from me. I claim back everything the devil has stolen from my family and me. I call back (name whatever the devil has stolen). I claim it all back multiplied by seven, in Jesus' name!

Now, let us return back to what I was sharing: There were other times when I'd hear snake sounds while sleeping. One night a snake attacked me, but I grabbed it by the head. It wrapped itself around my body. Then, I took it by the head, and ran outside and threw it as far as I could throw it and spoke, "I cast you into the abyss in Jesus' name!" If only I had a sword or knife to cut off the enemy's head! Whatever came up out of me is what I spoke but now I say, "I cast you into the **black hole** in Jesus' name!" Can a **black hole** kill you? According to theory, within a black hole there's something called a singularity. A singularity is what all the matter in a black hold gets crushed into. It might be turbulent, twisted, or any other number of things. One thing for sure, though: the tidal forces would kill you.

In 2012, right before I awakened in a dream, I saw a black snake like spirit flow out of my living room towards the front door and went out under the door. I believe God did a cleansing in my home. I really feel as though someone had been speaking cursed words or doing evil against me. So, I asked God to reveal the truth so that I could deal with the root of the matter. One thing for sure, someone was doing evil against me and the truth would be revealed. These events kept happening and all I could do is what I knew: plead the blood of Jesus over myself as well as my home. It would leave, but different episodes would occur. I'd ask, "Lord, what am I missing here?" I would take authority over the witchcraft in Jesus' name. I always knew it was witchcraft because that much was revealed to me by God.

It was June 2012; an evangelist came to our church. His message was, "Kill It or It Will Kill You." He said, "You've got to kill it before it grows. God has given you the opportunity to kill it. You can have all the hands laid on you that you want but, unless you decide today that things are going to die, it will abide and destroy you. The enemy steals from you and your children. Let it die! It's bondage in your life, kill it, kill it now!" After service, I ran home to pray. I took authority over the witchcraft spirit and commanded it to go to the feet of Jesus. Each door post and windows were anointed with blessed oil as I open the window to cast out the spirit of witchcraft.

That next morning the spirit of fear was gone off of my life and I believe to this day God allowed me to go through this to help others that come across my path. Yes, fear was gone off my life the very next day. I sense a sword in my right hand in the spirit to cut off the head of the enemy. Praise God! Please don't get me wrong; God doesn't place evil on anyone but if you open a door of sin for example, the enemy will come in like a flood, so repent! People destroy themselves because they don't want to get rid of their own sin and in some cases, people sometimes just need help just as I did because they don't know how to get free. We want to shout but we don't want to feel any pain. If we don't put our issues to death, they can kill us. In other words, deal with your issues.

It was still 2012, I met a friend at church, whose name was Lydia, and we began to spend some time together. So, I asked Lydia if she'd come to my house and pray with me to sense if anything was there that shouldn't be. She said, "Yes." She went from room to room praying and then sat in my brand-new La-Z-Boy chair that I'd bought for my husband at the time. Lydia said, "This is your secret place of prayer. Move it in the office area of your home." Lydia and I moved the chair. Lydia also called me the next day and said, the Lord had shown her that something was on the boards under my mattress. She said that a spirit not of God needed to be prayed out of my house. When I got home from work, I begin a cleansing prayer. I had to gird myself up in the Holy Ghost and anointed myself with oil. I flipped the mattress and box springs, anointed the boards in the name of Jesus and took authority over the witchcraft spirit and commanding it to go! From there I opened the windows and cast out anything that was in my home that didn't belong. Again, I anointed the closets, bed, vents, computers, plugs, outlets, cell phone, house phone, doors, and anything else I felt led to anoint in Jesus' name! Every now and then a house cleansing sealed by the blood of Jesus is needed.

In 2013, I received word from someone that I met at church. She shared with me what the Lord had spoken to her. "God's going to give you a revelation of why you went through what you did." The words she spoke to me gave me hope.

My friend Donna came to see me at work and told me that she needed to share something with me. She told me that, Cote, a coworker, had been sticking pins in a voodoo doll on my behalf as well as the supervisor. I thanked her and told her, "I'll take it from here." When I got home, I went into serious prayer:

"Plead my cause, O Lord, with them that strive with me: fight against them that fight against me." Psalm 35:1

"Let them be ashamed and confounded together that seek after my soul to destroy it: let them be driven backward and put to shame that wish me evil." Psalm 40:14

I pleaded a bloodline between me and the witchcraft and said, "Spirit of witchcraft return to the sender on behalf of my supervisor and myself in Jesus' name." Layers of evil had been removed which took care of that particular situation, praise God! Later, I found out that Cote had been on sick leave and almost died. My prayers went out to him. Later that night as I was sleep in the midnight hour, I heard this in my spirit right before my eyes opened:

'Aim at the target, command it to go.'

"What is it?" I asked?

'Torment,' is what my ears heard.

"From whom," I asked?

'You know,' is what my spirit heard.

I said, "I command the tormenting spirit to go now in the name of Jesus!"

God was teaching me how to counteract the enemy!

At 3:00 one morning, I heard a rattle snake sound right next to me while sleeping. I quickly got up out the bed and spoke these words: "You are a tormenting spirit I command you to go in Jesus' name!" I got my anointing oil to anoint my bed as well as myself and went back to sleep. I contemplated, "Why am I having these issues Lord? I'm a little confused about all of this. You know I've never experienced such. All this evil is new to me and I don't like any of it. Lord, help me to understand all I've encountered." God gave me these following scriptures to use during my morning prayer:

11. Put on the whole armour of God, that ye may be able to stand against the wiles of the devil.

12. For we wrestle not against flesh and blood, but against principalities, against powers, against the rulers of the darkness of this world, against spiritual wickedness in high places

13. Wherefore take unto you the whole armour of God, that ye may be able to withstand in the evil day, and having done all, to stand.

14. Stand therefore, having your loins girt about with truth, and having on the breastplate of righteousness;

15. And your feet shod with the preparation of the gospel of peace;

16. Above all, taking the shield of faith, wherewith ye shall be able to quench all the fiery darts of the wicked.

17. And take the helmet of salvation, and the sword of the Spirit, which is the word of God:

18. Praying always with all prayer and supplication in the Spirit and watching thereunto with all perseverance and supplication for all saints; Ephesians 6:11-18 (KJV).

Early one morning as my eyes opened facing the nightstand, I saw in the spirit a big black spider. I begin to pray, "I bind the strongman of the occult which is under the Jezebel Spirit of witchcraft. From my generational bloodline on my mother's and father's side all the way back to Adam and Eve, I ask for forgiveness and that the curse be broken in Jesus' name by the power of the Holy Spirit that abides within me." I thought to myself, here I go again!

It was 5:00 AM, things just kept happening to me and I didn't know who or where to turn. Enough is enough with this foolishness! I wanted to just give up! Unbelievably while sleeping I dreamed that a dog, yes! a dog sat on top of my head and I couldn't move at all! It *was* witchcraft and someone *was* still sending evil my way and I didn't know how to stop it except to say, "I bind you tormenting spirit in the name of Jesus! I command you to go where the Lord Jesus sends you and I lose peace and rest." Then, I called on the ministering spirits of God to come and minister to me. Lord, I said to him, "I'm tired of all this evil attacking me. Help me understand why this is happening to me. Don't give up on me."

I awoke at 9 AM and felt as though something was crawling at the bottom of my left leg. It jarred me and felt very eerie. "The blood of Jesus!' I shouted out. "I command you to go and I roast you by the fire of God in Jesus' name!" Then, I proceeded to get my anointing oil to anoint my bed and my legs and went back to sleep. As I fell back to sleep, I kept feeling something on the left side of my head pushing and pulling upward and downward that felt similar to spider web strings. I began to command it to go in Jesus' name acknowledging God in my life. I anointed my head with oil and went back to sleep again. "Lord," I said, "What is this coming against me?" The Lord spoke to me and reminded me as I reflected on my behavior while watching the case on George Zimmerman. As I was watching the verdict of not guilty being made, I got mad and said, "He's guilty!" I had judged the man and gotten myself into trouble with God! I asked God to forgive me for judging. I realized I'm not the judge, God is the judge. So, I blessed Mr. Zimmerman by praying for his whole family as well as Trevon and his family. Take heed: it is better to be careful by not speaking about situations or people we do not know. God granted his mercy upon me as I asked to be restored; and He did!

November 20, 2013, the bloodline curse on my mother's side had been revealed to me through a dream and I knew it had to be broken. In the dream, my eyeballs were white all over. I begin rubbing them and the iris within my pupils came back in place. Then, I wiped them again and they became all white again. It was a scary situation. So, I asked God, "What is this? What does this mean?" I heard the Lord say to me, "Voodoo in your bloodline." Voodoo is a form of witchcraft. Now, witchcraft I knew was in my family bloodline, but I didn't know to what extent!

After God revealed this to me concerning my bloodline, I searched for a cleansing and repentance prayer. I listen to a CD called, "How to change your DNA" by Dr. Francis Miles. I also listened to, "Prayer for Generational

Blessings of Abraham." Thank you, Lord for coaching me towards my freedom.

You must keep reading because it seems no matter what was done in each situation in my natural mind nothing looked as though it worked but it was working because layers of junk were being removed whether it could be seen or not. *"For we walk by faith, not by sight." 2 Corinthians 5:7 (BSB)*

I had a dream: A lot of people and myself were inside of a building somewhere. A female ran right up to me and snatched what I had out of my hand and proceeded to run away with my item. I ran after that heifer (as I said to myself) as fast as I could to catch her. As I was running, it came to my mind that my purse was not with me. So, I turned around to run back to get my purse, and it was still there on the floor. I grabbed my purse and began to run after her as fast as I possibly could. Up the flight of stairs, I ran. A group of people that were standing at the top of the stairs were looking upset as I passed by because that same female stole items from them as well. I saw them but did not stop to talk. I ran absolutely right pass them to catch her. Then, I woke up.

Interpretation: The female represents the enemy, who comes to steal from us, but we don't even recognize him for the most part. We blame others for our own downfalls instead of looking at the one that steals, kills, and destroys. ***"The thief comes only to steal and kill and destroy." John 10:10a (ESV).*** My purse represented identity. The enemy stole many things from me, but no more! What God has given me must be treasured as if it's gold. Yet we are far more valuable than gold. God created us in his image and likeness. Hallelujah!

On August 4, 2013, I woke up hearing snake sounds. "Oh Lord!" I said. "What in the world is going on now? I cast you to the abyss in the name of Jesus!" What happened was two females on my job had been giving me a hard time and I allowed it to stay on my mind with unforgiveness in my heart. It seemed like every time I'd take a step forward; I'd find myself being pushed two steps back. Because I had an unrepentant heart that opened a door to the enemy to attack me. It's necessary for me to be careful what I say out of my mouth. In prayer, I began to bless both of them. I sought God for help asking Him to let this pass from me. With a repentant heart I wanted to turn every negative situation at work around for good. As months went by, one of the female's home got broken into and a man climbed in her window and was standing over her when she opened her eyes. It was her next-door neighbor. He was sent off to jail. I believe prayer kept her from being harmed.

Did you know there's few deliverance ministries around, at least in my city? Many churches don't want to get their hands dirty when it comes to warfare to say the least. It also could be from fear or just being unlearned. God was teaching me how to war in my sleep-in time of need, along with worshipping Him. He would also show me what the enemy was doing behind my back. For example: While sleeping I could hear someone speaking evil words against me. Most of the time I recognized their voice. He taught me to keep Him as the center of my life that I may stay focused on him and not the enemy. God also taught me to be fearless. It seemed like every time I'd go for deliverance; God would reveal to me strongholds from my youth (as a child) that needed to be broken. Each time a situation was revealed to me I would get help so that I could receive my freedom (healing).

If there's a demonic spirit causing the problem in your life say, "I command you in the name of Jesus to go!" You are not trapped in a situation from which there's no escape: never lose hope in Jesus. ***"Resist the devil, and he will flee." James 4:7 (KJV).*** Without His power nothing is going to happen. We need His power because the enemy won't listen to your flesh therefore, it's all about being equipped with the Spirit of God.

There is another way to counteract through prayer. Learn to pray excessively in the spirit (tongues). Pray in the spirit for at least 30 minutes to break off what's on you. If you don't have the baptism of the Holy Spirit get someone that can help you get filled with the evidence of speaking in other tongues (heavenly language) by the laying on of hands through prayer. But, if you don't believe, just believe. It's all a faith walk anyway.

August 30, 2015, I asked God how long I had to suffer in this manner. I needed deliverance. Deliver me! This was revealed to me in my spirit: When Jesus was in the garden of Gethsemane he prayed, ***"Father, if you are willing, take this cup of agony away from me. But no matter what, your will must be mine." Luke 22:42 (TPT)***

God was revealing to me that Jesus suffered instead of complaining. He prayed to the Father, so I likewise could do the same. I was emphatically sure that He would always be with me. This was my training ground so that I could pull others out of ditches. I had to become small, so He could become big. This is when I truly realized that God was in total control of this ordeal no matter what I had endured. "Lord," I said, "My life's in your hands."

My friend from Columbus, Ohio called me to share a dream she had concerning me: I, Deborah, was sitting in a room and blood was forming around my feet. My arms were surrendered in the air. With tears streaming down my face I began saying, "Yes Lord, your will, not my own will." Blood begin running down the walls and I stepped out of grayish clothing (grave clothes) and new clothes appeared on me. Then, I begin to dance before the Lord and the blood begin to surround me as I danced. God showed me that no matter the circumstance you're covered with the blood of Jesus, rest assured. Hallelujah!

It was summertime on a Saturday afternoon, so I decided to get my sketch pad and pencils out to go downtown on the riverbank to sketch. It gave me such peace and serenity just being around the water. Kids were running around, and drunk men were laying in the grass asleep. So, I began to pray for the men. You never know, they may not even have a place to call home. Prayer is always the key to everything in our lives. To be honest, I prayed a prayer that someone would come by and say, "Thus said the Lord…" to bless and help me shed more light on my own troubles. It was a hope and wish that never happened, bless God!

Refuge House

In 2012, I went to visit a church called Refuge House where Pastor Cletus was the overseer. I felt the presence of the Lord therefore, I made it my home. During altar call Pastor Cletus anointed all who came for prayer. He anointed my head, laid hands on my shoulder, back and neck. I felt the warmth of God in his hands. He walked away and came back to pray for me silently. I began to grab him around his waist and just held on for dear life. That's how desperate I was to be free from it all. I thanked the Lord for using someone that could discern the Spirit of God and my need for help at such a time. Then, he had a young lady to come pray for me. She did and she began to holler out again and again as loud as she could. Deliverance had finally come! It went on for about eight seconds, I believe. My heart was so blessed and grateful to God that this day of deliverance had come. We both hugged while she asked, "What's your name?" I told her my name. As I returned to my seat, I kneeled down to the floor crying while thanking God for my healing. After service, I went to Pastor Cletus to ask him why was the lady that prayed for me hollering so loudly. He told me that stress and frustration was released from me. God knows what we need at the right time, bless God! This was just the beginning of the deliverance that I needed. As I stated before, Refuge House was the beginning of my journey where I stayed for 5 years.

As I continued coming to Refuge House, I'd go to the soaking room to soak. The soaking room is a place where people can meditate and offer prayers to God. I said to God, "This is just what I need because I love soaking and meditating before you Lord." One day as I was in the room soaking and minding my own business a man tapped me on the shoulder and told me, "The Lord said, you're to go to Mexico with that group of people sitting over there." I told him, "I'll pray about it because He hasn't said anything to me." He said, "OK." In my mind, speaking to myself I said, "I'm going through some issues here and need to be delivered, what is he talking about?" Two weeks later God showed me a dream where I was to go to Mexico with a group that I didn't know; after all, I was a new member.

Before I went to Mexico, I had set an appointment with Pastor Cletus so that he knew what I was going through and to cry out for help. All of this was new to me and more than I could handle. Therefore, using wisdom I thought I'd get some help. While counseling with Pastor he got down on one knee and prayed for me, but I needed more than prayer but deliverance in which I didn't receive.

The man was right. Later I went with the group to Campeche, Mexico. This was my first missionary trip. It was very exciting for me because I didn't know what to expect. This is how God showed me part of my destiny in life. We were in Mexico for about nine days. We went from one Church to another speaking, sharing, loving, giving and fellowshipping. However, I was still going through my own ordeal. Every service we went to blew me away. The Spirit of God engulfed us, and a miracle occurred! Gold dust appeared in peoples' hair, on their hands and on the floor. During worship they told me my eyes looked like a 50-cent piece. I was amazed at the manifestation that occurred. These people were used to seeing gold dust! A young lady told me that sometimes they had to get a broom and sweep the gold dust up off the floor! In silence, I said to myself, "I should've brought a mason jar to collect some of this." I marveled, "Why would God allow me to go to Mexico?" I was the one that needed help. God allowed me to see His glory and His presence on a deeper level. He allowed me to see what real love looks like and also allowed me to know there's more to him than what I've ever experienced. God had allowed me to know him in a greater facet through His love.

After returning from Mexico in 2013, I met a new friend named Karla. She was a teacher in the word of God at Refuge House. She also started a Bible study in her lovely home on Thursdays and I was happy to attend. The fellowship was great! Karla was so generous that she'd buy the books for Bible study. It was a joy attending classes and meeting new people from outside of our church.

One day, as the group was having Bible study in Karla's home, there was a red bird pecking on the window of her living room. I said, "Karla there's a bird on your windowpane that won't go away." She said, "Yes I know, it's been coming day and night." "How long has it been pecking on your window?" I asked. She said, "For a little while." I told her that she should go pray to God and find out why." She said, "I've been asking already." The following week during study the red bird was there again, but in the dining room window instead. "I see that red bird is back," I said. "You should pray and ask God to see if he's trying to tell you something." I proceeded to tell her my testimony that occurred during my second marriage: "Some years ago, when I arrived home there was a robin pecking on my window. My ex-husband, Vernard, told me "That dumb bird has been pecking on the window all day." I told him it was because God has been waiting on me to come home and had a message for me. Vernard told me I was crazy along with the bird. As I looked at the robin in the window, I asked God, "What do you need to tell me Lord?" Before I went to bed, I prayed asking God to reveal to me what He wanted to tell me. The very next day, which was Sunday, the robin came back pecking on the same window around 8:00 AM in the living room. I pulled back the curtain as I was getting ready for church. While looking at the robin in his eyes I said, "Lord, what is it that you want to share with me?" The Spirit of God spoke to me and said, "I have freed you this day." The Lord had already spoken to me concerning Vernard. The bird's frequent visitation was a confirmation of what I should do. He told me to tell him to stop sinning and lying about it. Vernard didn't believe me yet he knew what he was doing was wrong. Now, you understand why God gave me revelation through the robin that kept pecking on the window. I told Vernard that God had set me free from the marriage because of his refusal to change his lifestyle. Yet, he said to me once again, "You're crazy just like that bird." Not many months later, I moved out and went through a cleansing in mind, spirit, soul and body. *"Whom the son sets free is free indeed." John 8:36*

Since I had the experience with the robin, I was able to minister to Karla in the Bible group. I told her to really pray and find out what massage God wanted to share with her and to find out if it was God. She didn't believe it was God and some of the other ladies didn't believe it either. I kept telling her to pray about it. I couldn't believe it! I was shocked at their response that's when I stopped coming to the Bible studies. Now, don't get me wrong in what I'm saying: they had been praying for me because I told them I was irritated around my eyes and really wondered if someone was speaking or even doing any witchcraft against me. I had to plead the blood of Jesus over myself as well as anoint my eyes with blessed oil in Jesus' name! I still needed deliverance from the swarming around my eyes *(it felt like nets irritating my eyes)*. It was a spiritual battle. I asked, "God, what's going on around my eyes?" It went on for a while and I kept praying to get understanding. The scripture says in *Proverbs 4:7b (KJV) "…therefore get wisdom: and with all thy getting get understanding."* After much prayer it finally went away. Praise God!

In 2015, I had taken myself through a self-deliverance on CD as instructed by Nick Griemsmann. I dealt with the junk that I knew about: unforgiveness, witchcraft spirit, tormenting spirit, pride, negative word curses, control, and manipulation which were stemming from my bloodline.

In October 2016, I heard in my sleep, "black magic" and the root "divination." I began to research prayers online for *"the root of divination and black magic." It was my intent to find out how to destroy these evil works in my family's bloodline.* This is the prayer I prayed:

Prayer: Father, forgive me and my family bloodline for any past or current involvement in any cultic activities. I love you God and want to live a life that's pleasing to you. Satan, in the name of Jesus' I bind you and the spirit of divination according to **Matthew 18:18, which clearly states, "whatsoever you shall bind on earth shall be bound in heaven."** *Consider any pact that was made either by me or my family in the past to be broken once and for all. You have no hold on my life or my family from now on in the name of Jesus. Thank you, Lord Jesus', for freeing me and I worship you. I lose the power of the Holy Spirit in*

I released the anointing, the manifestation of gifts of the spirit, prophetic anointing, the apostolic anointing of Elijah, the anointing of Jehu on my life in Jesus' name. Amen!

While I was still at Refuge House an unfortunate event occurred. One afternoon, I was on my way to church. It was intercessory day to pray for Israel. When I got in the parking lot, I sat in my car finishing my sandwich. While having my head down biting on the sandwich one of the men from the church began driving around encircling my car several times. The man eventually drove away to another part of the lot and parked. I felt very uncomfortable because first of all he was married. Nearby a couple got out of their car and saw what he was doing. I got out of my car and went into the church. When I got into the church, I heard the couple telling his wife what they had seen. I felt so bad for his wife because I hadn't done any- thing. A week or two later Pastor Cletus said out loud during service, "Up there messing with somebody's husband." I said to the Lord, "I know darn well he's not talking about me." He said it as I was coming up to the altar to pray. Another lady and I had come to the altar to pray. It was just two of us that came forth. I began looking at her wondering if it was, she. But no, he was pointing the finger at me. In prayer at the altar to God I said, "Lord, the truth will set them free indeed!" There wasn't anything for me to say to them because I wasn't guilty, not even a little. Therefore, I let the negative words roll right off me and I kept moving. I learned a valuable lesson: Don't allow untruths to pull you down. That's what the enemy wants for you. Gird yourself up, put your armor on and release all the negative thoughts from your mind. Free yourself!

At this time, I was still at Refuge House, but I was not working in the church. I was just attending services, Bible study and intercessory prayer (which I love)! I'd just gotten my 501C3 and my plan was to obtain a house like setting where I could start an after-school program helping younger females and sharing the word of God with them. But after I received the 501C3 it seemed as if nothing worked out financially to fulfill my vision. One November day I decided to go to a local grocery store to ask for turkey donations being that it was near Thanksgiving. It was laid on my heart to try and do this for the less fortunate. I received turkeys and gave ten to Pastor Cletus to bless others. Also, I had ten to pass out in the community. I was also given gift cards from a few businesses which I gave to the pastor to distribute. I thought all was well, but something happened in the midst of giving that shifted our relationship. I visited several stores to pick up the gift cards. When I got to the last store, the manager said, someone from the church had already picked up the gift card. Later, at the church I explained the situation to a leader. The leader said, he had sent someone to pick up the card instead of me. I felt the pastor didn't trust me! Everything went downhill from there. Needless to say, I never dealt with handing out turkeys or gift cards again. That was the end of that for me!

Additionally, while still at Refuge House I experienced an issue concerning my pastor's wife of whom I loved dearly! I was on the phone with a church member, Bee, (sad to say). I made one of the biggest mistakes of my life. I was sharing with her my thoughts concerning the women's gatherings of which my Pastor's wife was the overseer. If I could turn back the hands of time it surely would've never happened. Anyway, I shared that we should have the women's gatherings more often thinking if we had them more often maybe God would heal the Pastor's wife sooner than later. I learned that sharing this thought was a BIG mistake! Bee ran with this information; taking it back to the Pastor and or his wife as soon as she could. She'd hurt them both and I'd hurt them by sharing this with Bee. I should've kept my mouth shut and my thoughts to myself! I'd offended them with my words, but can you blame them? I felt so bad for running my mouth. I learned a valuable lesson, don't loosely talk about the leaders! Be constructive and wise with whom you share.

Shortly after, I felt it was time for me to move on. I had been there five years. I felt moving was a good idea. I left Refuge House in 2016. After leaving, I stayed home for six months and just visited churches occasionally. All I did was study the word until God instructed me otherwise. I paid tithes wherever I was led to attend church each month. Whoever fed me with the word of God, that's where my tithes were sown, besides it's Gods money. My mother taught our family to pay our tithes when we got our first jobs and I never stopped.

Dead Man Walking

October 16, 2016

This is a dream I've encountered with six different rooms and occurrences happening one after another. It seems as though I was watching myself as a character in a movie, but no one could see me.

Room number 1 – I saw two females that I knew, Sasha and Alisha. They were just standing there looking as if not knowing where to go. One of them walked off to see what she could see. Neither of them saw me as I walked right past them and said, "Hi." Yet, Sasha just stood there looking.

Room number 2 - In the next room were people with all black on. I didn't feel as though I belonged and really didn't want to see what was happening. I felt as though they were attending a funeral, but who died? I wondered if it was me that died.

Room number 3 – There were three females at the front desk looking so sad and one of them was my oldest sister, the other two were her friends. My sister had on a white winter coat looking brilliant with a glow. They were all glowing!

Room number 4 – Here, I opened a door to a room that had different items for sale. So, I bought a brown purse there. Also, dresses and clothes were on the floor. I spoke out loud and said, "This room has been changed." It seemed to look like a storeroom. Again, no one saw me yet I could see them.

Room number 5- Here in this dream my one and only son was laying on the floor with a friend that I didn't know. They were having sex with a brilliant white blanket covering them. It seemed as though they were in an open space, not really a closed room. My eyes couldn't believe what I was seeing, and I said to the Lord, "Am I dead here?" Then fear came upon me and I didn't know what to do.

Event number 6: Later, I gave my son a ride from the same place where all the different events occurred. But we never even talked (as if I wasn't there). I came back to the place where I bought the brown purse because I realized my purse wasn't with me. But when I got back to the place, I couldn't find it. I saw my sister and her two friends still in the main hall. They were very serious and sad. I said, "Hi," but they didn't hear nor see me. In my spirit I realized that they were at my funeral. It blew me away so much that all I could do was look and look and look. Fear gripped me more than anything because no one could see me. "Lord, am I really dead? Where am I? Oh, God help me because I don't know what to do here. Why am I seeing this?" That's when I really realized I was a "Dead Man Walking."

When I woke from the dream, I began to pray and ask God to forgive me for anything I had done wrong. I also ask God to forgive those who had done me wrong. I wanted God to bless and release each one of them including some family members. Yes, in Jesus' name!

Now let's talk about these rooms I just shared with you:

Room Number 1 – Sasha and Alisha at that time were standing around just looking to see. I felt the two were present to see more so than really care. After all, these two females were the only ones not glowing like some of the others.

Room number 2 - The room with people in all black were at a funeral which I truly believe was mine. This represents dying to the flesh. I had been asking God to kill my flesh; little did I know I was experiencing it.

Room number 3 - The three females (my sister and her two friends) were coming to my funeral glowing. This represented the true church of Jesus Christ.

Room number 4 - The closet with the clothes and purses represented my identity, as though I forgot who I was in Christ. I was feeling as though I wasn't victorious emotionally. The enemy had stolen from me, but no more!

Room number 5 - My one and only son was lying on the floor with a brilliant white blanket covering the two of them while having sex, represented myself praying and covering him regardless of how he's living right now. I know he's coming back to Jesus. Your past doesn't dictate what your future will be. ***"For I know the thoughts I think toward you, says the LORD, thoughts of peace and not of evil, to give you a future and a hope." Jeremiah 24:11 (NKJV)***

Don't allow the enemy to steal your identity. Without knowing who you are, it's like a *dead man walking* such as I went through. You're just barely surviving not knowing who you are in God. That's exactly what happened. Know who you are because Satan doesn't have any new tricks. He's using the same tactics he's been using for over 2000 years. My problem was I blamed others instead of myself or the enemy. Once you get to the root of the matter, you'll realize it wasn't the other person at all for the most part. Then, who could it be? 1). The enemy is using you; or 2). God allows the door to be opened for the enemy to come in because of the sin in your life. Therefore, we must repent and ask God to forgive us and turn away from our sins.

Death from Within

Dr. Karen Looman, D.O. explained decomposition to me: "The body releases an odor that attracts insects such as blow flies and will smell the decomposing body. They come into the body and lay eggs in warm moist areas; like the corners of your eyes, nose and mouth if it's open, and arm pits. Any holes in the body of any kind, the flies will lay eggs. Also, when the eggs hatch, they become maggots. The maggots eat the flesh of the body as well. Therefore, decomposition is smelly, a horrible smell. "Our physical body is similar to a piece of meat once the soul leaves the body. It will decay just like meat left on a counter. Your body slowly starts to break down. The cells in your intestines and lungs breakdown. Bacteria in your blood system starts creating gases, a byproduct of the bacteria. You develop gas in the body."

I have to be honest about the situation that I'm about to share because it's a part of what I had to endure but with much embarrassment. My whole body literally stunk from inside out. These were the parts of my body that let off a really deadly, smelly scent. I know it sounds unreal but it's true.

* Through breathing-one could literally smell my bad halitosis.

* Odor from body parts.

* Breaking wind - which sounded as if it was an animal: deadly smells.

* Pores - smells came even through my pores.

* Places around my eyes, mouth, and fingertips. It felt as if blowflies were swarming around them.

The odor was a very deadly throw off. If you sat next to me, you could smell that something wasn't right. In fact, one day in service the lady I was sitting next to even said somethings wasn't right. I was so embarrassed to say the least.

What you just read; these are the things I've encountered while dying from within, not knowing really what was happening within my own being. This went on for a couple of years. I began taking soaking baths with natural oil's and such. I thank God for keeping me while going through my process and continuing in the word of God no matter the cost and embarrassment. Prayer is the key to every situation in life I must say: it's my lifeline to the ultimate source, Jesus!

God taught me in all of this to do whatever you can to help someone along the way. There's a scripture that says, ***"Be not deceived; God cannot be mocked: for whatsoever a man soweth, that shall he also reap."*** ***Galatians 6:7 (KJV)*** What a man sows he will also reap… in return. Don't be afraid to ask someone in need, "Is there anything I can do for you?" Had anyone asked me this question, believe you me, my response would've been a resounding "Yes!" You never know who God will allow you to come across their path to receive help. ***"Ask, and the gift is yours. Seek, and you'll discover. Knock, and the door will be opened for you." Matthew 7:7 (The Passion Translation)***

Beth Messiah

December 11, 2016 I heard while sleeping, "Go find a Rabbi (teacher) and ask him to bless you." I didn't hear a name, but I felt God wanted me to explore the Jewish roots of faith. That's what happened. On January 1, 2017, I found Beth Messiah online. It's the only Holy Ghost, Spirit filled, Jewish congregation in Ohio, which was about 22 minutes from my home. And yes, I did ask Rabbi to bless me. He blessed me on the day we met. The thought of the initial encounter even makes me smile to this day.

As I begin to go to Bible study on Saturday mornings before Sabbath, I discovered the teachings were very clear and more broad-spanned than the norm. I learned about the holy days of worship. The way Beth Messiah congregants honored God with communion, dancing before the Lord, and reading the Torah was amazing to me. I felt as though I was in Israel. In fact, I went to Israel twice and learned so much concerning the ways of Jewish culture. What I really love about the Jewish culture is that they take God very seriously like I've seen in many other cultures. It was truly a blessing to have fellowship with them for the six months God had me there to learn. What an honor it was to go to their yearly conference in Philadelphia. Jews came from all over the world. It was amazing!

God gave me a dream letting me know I was released to leave after the conference was over. "I thought, "I just got here!" But, on the last day of the conference after class the Jewish speaker from Israel asked if anyone would like prayer before leaving. I got in line and he said, "Your time is up you already know." That was my confirmation to leave. Now, that blew me away. When we got back from the conference, before the next service, I went to see Rabbi M. to let him know it was time for me to leave. He didn't know at first but seemed a little disappointed, maybe, but I wasn't sure. Yet, he placed his hand on my shoulder and said, "Bless you." He walked away and continued doing what he needed to do before service started. I love those people! One more thing that really blessed me: being invited into a Jewish person's home for Bible study and having the Lord's Holy Communion with them on Sundays for me was an honor. Even Passover Seder which includes reading, having communion, telling stories, eating special foods, singing and other Passover traditions were such precious experiences for me. Thanks for inviting me into your home Sister Lois and Brother Levi with community! It's been an honor and a privilege.

Vinedresser

July 2018, I joined Vinedresser and what I loved about this house was the available training for anyone. There's much training available if one wants to learn, so there are no excuses for anyone not to grow and move forward in God as well as finding a place in the body to serve. That's what it's all about. Serve others as if you're serving God but do it in humility and with grace.

I had been studying about the body of Christ at large. The following information is taken from the book entitled, "The Body of Christ," by Watchman Nee which explains how Satan divides the body. Nee states:

Satan's Work of Disintegration

"We ought to know that in order to spread His gospel, do His work, and fulfill His will on earth, the Lord must use His body. Neither His will nor His way can be realized through one person, since the Lord does not work through one man but through the church. The life and power of Christ find their richest manifestation through the body of Christ. For this reason, Satan takes great pains to try to affect the "disintegration" of the body of Christ. This becomes his number one task. If we take note of this, we will readily realize how severe is this Satanic work of "disintegration:" suspicion arises among brothers and sisters, misunderstanding is easily created. This is Satan doing his disintegrating work. One of us is blaming a brother, and the latter is murmuring against a sister. Yet, if the cause is investigated, there is nothing serious about it at all. This too is Satan performing his work of tearing down the body. The work of God is to make us one body, but the work of Satan is to cause us to be torn asunder. But it rests upon the fact that it is Satan who use these weaknesses of ours to do the work of tearing and dividing. By the filtering of the cross and the Holy Spirit, we have but one need, which is, to turn inwardly to God and allow Him to cleanse us and purify us with the cross and the Holy Spirit. We hope and pray we may be cleansed from all the impurities which Satan has mixed into us." Quoted from Watchman Nee, The Body of Christ: A Reality. *[New York: Christian fellowship publisher 1978] pp. 46-49.* Used by permission.

Things Gone Wrong

I'm sure many people in the body of Christ have been hurt and left churches. In all the circumstances I have endured in my life, this deeply felt hurt has made me stronger than ever before.

Kingdom Ministry was a ministry that I enjoyed participating in. Pastor Jim was the teacher of Kingdom Ministry. His parents Pastor Virgil and mother Clara were the overseers of Vinedresser Ministries.

We were in our Kingdom Ministry class and our leader, Pastor Jim, asked some of us to come up and share our experiences as we ministered to people in different locations in the community. As I came up front to share, I happened to turn my head to the left towards Pastor's way and he gave me a look as though he was not impressed with anything I was saying. Therefore, I wouldn't look his way again.

Whatever was shared with Pastor Virgil concerning myself changed the way he looked at me. What do I mean by this statement? All of a sudden, I'd be near the pastor; he would either not speak or look at me in a cold way.

Being that I hadn't been there but a short time, I felt it was important to ask Pastor Jim if we could meet so that he would know what I was going through during the time of his class. The scripture encourages leaders to be familiar with their flock. It states the following: ***"And we beseech you, brethren, to know them that labor among you, and are over you in the Lord, and admonish you;" I Thessalonians 5:12 (KJV).*** Therefore, I went to him to ask if we could meet and his response was, "I don't meet with females." I re-phrased, "I meant you and your wife; that's how it should be." Pastor Jim said, "I'll think about it." That left me confused because it was made clear that I didn't want to just meet with him alone, but his wife as well. It was never mentioned again. I brushed off his indifferent response concerning me like water on a duck's back and kept on moving forward.

Mitch is over the prophetic class entitled, "Be Holy." He would share with the entire class, then we'd get into our groups to further discuss the topic. One week before the last class, Mitch had gone around and ministered to some of the body. He came to me and said, "They don't want you…" He wouldn't finish and left the rest off. Then, he proceeded to minister to me regarding me having a testimony. To be honest, I was messed up behind what was said, but I was trying to hide my feelings. The female sitting right behind me must've heard what Mitch said because she came to me and embraced me as if it was Jesus' arms around me. God heard me as I said within myself, "I need a hug." Mitch made me feel so bad and I'm grateful to God for how he used the young lady. Anyway, all I wanted to do was finish up the class and that's what I did.

Later, I found out why Pastor Virgil, the overseer, became indifferent with me. Mitch who was over the "Be Holy" class ministered to me at the altar one Sunday right after service. I made a big mistake by letting him know my personal business so he could pray and minister to me about the matter. I was very satisfied with him ministering to me. However, Mitch shared my personal business with all that were in the leadership meeting. One of the leaders shared with me this piece of information. In addition, someone who got hold of my personal information spread my business with some of the body. Some of the members began to treat me indifferent as if I harmed someone. I couldn't believe those sweet ladies at the information desk became indifferent with me as well. It was warfare on my end to say the least, to pray heavily because of the indifference and rejection that I was experiencing.

I did address what Mitch said to me with another leader and she asked me if I'd like Mitch to meet with us. So, I said, "Yes." He did respond and said he wanted all three of us to meet. All I wanted him to do was apologize for what he said. I thought, *what happened to integrity these days? God expects us to be people of integrity; people who keep our word, honor our agreements and fulfill our obligations. If God can forgive those who crucified Him surely, we can forgive those who trespass against us. Forgiveness is a matter of the heart. Mitch said he wasn't going to apologize because he didn't say, "they don't want you..." Regardless, he is forgiven.*

I learned through this experience that it's unwise to openly share intimate issues with people we don't know spiritually. Instead, we must learn to go to God in prayer consistently and fervently. God in response will answer! He will send help for you to make it through. Thank you, Jesus!

These are the situations that allowed my faith in
God to become stronger in the area of love. Some may
wonder how such hurt and pain can produce growth in the
area of loving one another. Some may feel hatred towards
the ones that hurt them. But no, I know where my help
comes from. God has created us to love. Love will take you
places your mind can't comprehend. What I'm trying to say
is that love will keep your heart and motives in line with
the word of God if you allow it. In order to keep our hearts
right we must stay in repentance mode, no matter the cause.
From there, keep moving forward. Forgiveness is one of
the most important commands we must do!

PEACE

The Lord spoke to me March 27, 2019.
"Forgiveness is the key to unlocking doors into your future.
Peace is where it presents itself no matter where it resides.
Your soul is a counterpart of your spirit that lies from
within. If you desire peace, rest in it that it may overtake
your consciousness. Make it a blanket for comfort over
your soul. Feel it, embrace the peace as a magnet on your

refrigerator. Peace will take you whereas your flesh causes the opposite-trouble." *Deborah Lynn 1-21-19*

Zoe Ministries

One afternoon as I was driving, Pastor Marcia came to mind that owns a Christian bookstore. When I pulled into the parking lot all the stores were vacant. I hadn't seen Pastor Marcia in about seven years. I really wanted to see her. When I got home, I looked up her number online to call her but there was no answer, so I left her a message. The very next day she returned my call and we were able to set up an appointment to meet. To make a long story short, I began attending her church, Zoe Ministries in January 2019. I also wanted to move forward to the next level in Christ, so I was really excited about attending her deliverance ministry.

What I loved about the ministry was that it bought about deliverance whereas in many, many churches one can receive prayer but that's it. Yet, some people need deliverance. It's sad to say, but a lot of churches are afraid and don't want to be taught nor trained. Some don't want to deal with the junk in your trunk, nevertheless, get their hands dirty. The Lord said, greater works will we do. Why aren't most churches doing it? My prayer is that the body of Christ step up to the plate and *BELIEVE* what the word of God says.

Pastor Marcia would preach the word of God and when she got done, the body would repeat after her the warfare prayer that was spoken to us out loud. We would make sure that repentance was one of the first things we prayed about. There were different prayers offered depending on what the message was or what was going on at the time (what the Lord would lay on Pastor Marcia's heart). But no matter what the reason was it was much needed for that particular time. One would leave refreshed. Besides, I needed prayer while still going through my ordeal.

Several weeks went by and Pastor Marcia had been absent from service. I asked her husband, Pastor Elijah, where she was and that's when he told the church that she was out of town. As weeks went by, I asked Pastor Elijah again about Pastor Marcia. He told the church that she was still out of town. I began to get a little concerned in my spirit. When she got back home and came to church, nothing was said (at least not to me). The following month

Pastor Marcia went out of town for the next few weeks and nothing was said to the church. That's when I really got concerned. Finally, Pastor Elijah told the church that Pastor Marcia had been really sick. My heart was sad to hear of such and yes, we did pray for her. Sometimes, it's best to hold your personal business, trust God and not let everyone know of your trails. Pastor Marcia is now well praise God!

While still going through my situation even at Zoe Ministries, I was hoping to get my total freedom because I felt as though I was at the end of my rope and, that's exactly where I was. And, was wondering how long I had to carry this cross because it doesn't seem as if the end will come. "Oh Lord, I said. "Did you leave me?" It seems as though no one could handle what I was going through completely. God told me one day, "Get down on your knees when you repent." That's what I do now and will continue to do. Little by little He would give me tidbits of what He wanted me to do. He was teaching me to be obedient and fine tuning my spirit. One can be going through hell and God will give him something that has nothing to do with what he's going through. I learned this a long time ago to go with the flow and pray.

It's time to trust and let God be who He said he'll be in your life. Ask God to grant you strength for endurance and perseverance. Not all demonic afflictions come as a result of sinful behavior or from past unholy allegiances. God just may permit Satan to attack you for his own purposes. In the book of Job his life was in turmoil. Satan asked God for permission to test Job. He lost his health, wealth, and family. Job even cursed the day he was born, and his own friends doubted him! So, don't tell me God won't do it. Look at the evidence in *Job 1:1-22.*

Note: Just as the enemy has studied humans, we as a people should study Satan's tactics as well. He's jealous of us because he lost the greatest gift God gave him. What was the gift? He lost being the top-notch musician and was thrown out of heaven. He and his imps lost eternal life. That was his choice and now it's his problem. However, this is what he gained: *eternal hell fire and brimstone.* Keep moving forward – FREE YOURSELF. Read: *Ezekiel 28:12-19, Isaiah 14:12-15, Revelation 12:7-12.*

LIFE ETERNAL CHURCH

On July 2019, I joined Life Eternal Church. The overseers were Pastor Brew and his wife. The church was small, but the awesome teaching was a blessing to me. The people were warm and friendly. They believed women shouldn't wear pants, jewelry, make-up, nail polish, or even go to a hair salon, they felt you should look modest. Now, I believe a woman should look modest as well but really, it's just a 'tradition of men.' I went along with it because I didn't have anything to lose. Besides, I didn't mind getting rid of all that stuff anyway. So, I got rid of it all and really felt free. To be honest, I felt as though God was striping me from what other women do and wear. I've learned from a book Sister Brew had me to read that the wearing of jewelry really stems from Egypt. When the children of Israel were free to leave from slavery in Egypt to the promise land, they brought all the jewelry from there. I'm merely sharing this bit of information because this is what I was taught at this particular church. It's true that the jewelry was brought from Egypt but think about it, what if the children of Israel didn't bring any jewelry with them?

Would we really have jewelry today? That's just some food for thought. Nevertheless, I'm not judging anyone. Judge not, that ye be not judged. ***"For with what judgment ye judge, ye shall be judged: and with what measure ye mete, it shall be measured to you again." Matthew 7:1-2 (KJV)***

The thing is, I gave my *"will"* to God therefore, I'm not my own. There's a hymn in which the chorus says, "I surrender all…" Well, that's where I was at that point in my life. I thought, 'whatever God tells me to do, thats what I'm going to do no matter what the world says because I'm wrapped up, tied up, and tangled up in Jesus!'

Pastor and Sister Brew were very good leaders and serious about the word of God. I loved that about them. The word was alive when Pastor Brew spoke, and it kept the church alert with enthusiasm. I asked Sister Brew if there was anything, I could do in the kingdom by way of serving in the church. During our women's conference she told us to write down what we've done or were qualified to do and to give it to her. So, that's what I did. However, she never said anything to me, and I felt it was important to work in the kingdom as much as we could. One day, Pastor Brew told the entire body to get busy in the kingdom and stop sitting there looking pretty! After service, I went to Sister Brew and told her what pastor had said to the body because she was in the office counting money and didn't hear the challenge. She told me that some of the ladies would get mad if she was to put me in a position since I hadn't been there long. I said, "What?" Thats when I went to Pastor Brew and told him what she said to me. He looked at me like, "What?" The following week after service I went to Sister Brew and she asked me why I told pastor what she had done. I told her because it's true. She was not happy with me, but she said, "It's okay." Yet, she never would put me in any position to work in the kingdom. Out of all the churches I've attended (and I've attended a lot), never, ever have I heard of such foolishness. What I've learned to this point is that the church is not yet ready to be His bride and that God is still working on all of us. Prayer is the key to every situation especially in the Body of Christ!

When I first joined Life Eternal Church, I didn't know anyone. Therefore, I had no idea that a young lady, whose name was Maranda, greeted newcomers and gathered information about the new person. She would call Pastor Brew and fill him in on what she was told. *For example,* if a newcomer had a bad spirit Miranda would call Pastor Brew on the phone and fill him in. Pastor would integrate the information into his sermon and the person could be led to think God was talking to her. I found out Maranda was doing this because a member of the church, Sister Sledge, told me. She said, "Sister Maranda tells pastor everything over the phone." I said to myself, "Hmmmm, people come to church to get a refilling, healed, delivered, set free, as well as yoke up with believers to build a closer relationship with God, not to be judged by man."

Another day we were at church for intercessory prayer. After prayer one of the ladies at the church told me in a sarcastic manner that they were praying about me giving items to some of the ladies at the church. She said that because I brought some items to church and gave them away. In turn, I asked her if she had gotten a response from God. She said, "Not yet." It seemed to be such a petty response to my wanting to give to others.

After another service, a young lady came up to me and asked if I went to a salon to get my hair done. I told her, "Yes." I said within myself, 'Don't you have anything

to say other than this being that we just got out of service?'
The following week she asked me the same question. I told
her that my niece came to my house and fixed my hair.
That killed that matter, she never asked again.

A couple of weeks later, I told Sister Brew,
"There's no place for me here and no need for me to stay."
For three months I wasn't allowed to do anything in the
church because she was afraid of what others might say
which could cause confusion. Pastor Brew had told all of us
to get busy. I was no longer going to just sit around doing
nothing. That was my clue to say goodbye. Sister Brew told
me there was room for me to serve and not to leave. She
also told me that I could always come back to *their*
church. That's when I knew for a surety it was time to
leave.

I felt rejected because of the negative interactions
from the church members. ***Rejection*** is a very dangerous
spirit that lingers in the body of Christ these days. I believe
to this day, that it's going to take a revival to come into the
churches so that God can give the body of Christ" a ***'blood
bath'*** to clean His church up!

Deep down in my heart I felt sorry for what happened that allowed these situations to occur. Yet, it taught me a valuable lesson: Its God's heart felt love that is the greatest gift for us no matter what happens in our lives. My request to the Lord was, "Help me to be a prime example to your people by allowing your liquid love to flow from heart to heart that I may please you even more." We only know we love Him by our love that we have for one another. My soul doth magnify the Lord!

The Final Curtain

"I was drowning in great sorrow because of the work of evil. When you feel as though you have no way out, there's always a detour which will be revealed to you somehow. It's funny how God allows us to do our own thing until we realize just how much we need Him. This is where I got stuck somewhere along the way. God wants to heal those wounds that's the work of evil. There is no pain free life! What you go through can sometimes work for your good. We allow it to consume us when we take our eyes off the one that created us." ***The Shack movie. Used by permission.***

Look at what happened to Jesus. His crucifixion is what set us free. *(Matthew 27:1-66, 28:1-20).* Jesus was crucified and buried. He rose again from the dead on the third day so that we might have a chance to the tree of life. Now, this is what love looks like. In other words, "Love just like you've never been hurt." That's exactly what Jesus did for all of us, but many don't realize just how much He suffered. Did he do it? YES, HE did!

Note: Whenever the Lord gives you a message whether it be a word for someone, instructions, or even to pray for someone, for example, run as fast as you can to fulfill it. Why? Because, obedience is the key to success. If God can trust you with something as small as this then He will trust you with much greater. All you have to do is *"Believe."* I've learned this from my very own experiences.

The word of the Lord was spoken to me by Prophet Dennis Cramer on March 16, 2018:

"Daughter, I'm letting you know what people have said about you and against you. Especially family that's been talking behind your back saying cruel and unusual things against you. Let it go! It's not true, you're not guilty. The Lord said, I erase all false charges against you. I wipe that slate clean. Now it's time to pick up the pace and continue the race that's before you. God said that the blessing of the Lord will come upon you. Now, this new season you're going to begin to draw upon your life's experience and they will be of great importance. Women will say, if you can make it, I can make it. You are an encourager, encourage my people. You are a woman with the power of God available in your hands. Lay your hand on people do your thing. And, do your job and you will get results."

On May 19, 2019, I heard that Prophet Welsh was coming to a church in Kentucky that afternoon. Prophet Welsh took the church through a repentance to clear the air for deliverance. God used Prophet Welsh to speak to me. He said, *"Look straight at me. God heard your prayer and you're not just healed but whole in Jesus' name."* I began to weep while thanking God for my freedom. Then, this story came to my mind. There were 10 men with leprosy. God healed all of them. But, as they went on their way, only one came back to bow down and say thank you. Jesus said to him, "Where are the rest?" That's when Jesus told him, ***"Arise and go. It was your faith that brought you salvation and healing." Luke 17:11-19 (TPT).*** I felt just like one of the ten lepers. The one that came back to say, *'thank you'* was the one that was made *whole.*

Also, I'd like to share with you my precious event that changed my life when I attended a life changer event:

Dallas, Texas

On October 4, 2019, I was blessed to have gone to a life changer annual event in Dallas, Texas called, "Yom Kippur." It is to honor *Day of Atonement,* which is a shadow of Jesus: *which emphasizes to hold a sacred assembly and deny yourself (Leviticus 23:27)*. After hearing the teaching so that all may have full understanding concerning Yom Kippur, we got baptized the next day. Everyone got baptized (not the same baptism when you get saved). This baptism happens once a year for a renewing of the Holy Spirit, sealing unlimited blessings over our lives, renewing of the mind, and opening the windows of heaven. Curses are broken off our family line that the enemy has put on us and we claim joy. Jesus died and took every curse and hung it on the tree, but we have to break the curse ourselves also by saying it. Just like when Jesus died on the cross for our sins, we still have to confess it with our mouth. That's why the same issues kept occurring with me even after getting prayer while going through the different events which were related to witchcraft. Confession of the mouth causes you to get saved and free. But I wanted to be more than healed just like the woman with the issue of blood. She crawled on her knees trying to touch the hem of Jesus' garment. She said to herself, "If I can but touch the hem of his garment then I know I'll be made whole." It was the same with me. Yes, I was healed at the church I visited in Kentucky on May19, 2019 but, I needed to be made whole from that witchcraft/tormenting spirit that was in my bloodline and whatever my ex-husband was carrying that was attached to me. It had to be destroyed in order for it not to flow down to my son and grandchildren along with my entire family. That's when the curses in my bloodline were broken off me and my family bloodline, praise God! I'm so grateful to God that He allowed me to attend this event for such a time as this.

It was an amazingly beautiful experience being baptized in this manner. After coming up out the water we are to expect to hear God even more. It's like being separated and born again like a new child. We are leaky vessels, so we need to get refilled with the Holy Spirit. I've heard people in the world say, "You can't change." But your issues can be broken by the Blood of Jesus. He died and broke our curses, any curses. There's no sickness the blood can't cover. God *will* raise up a standard. Besides, we must know who we are in Him. ***For in him we live, move, and have our being; Acts 17:28a (KJV)***

I'm currently not attending church until I receive notice from my Lord and Savior Jesus Christ. I have so many questions. Why did God allow me to attend all these different churches? Why did I have to go through all these occurrences? Was it to see how I handled these matters or to allow hurt in each situation? Absolutely not! As time passes, I continue to ask the Lord what was this all about. God allowed me to see what was going on in some of the churches at large. He helps me to see how there's more of serving the flesh and less of Him. God also allows me to understand that His church will be without spot or wrinkle before it's all said and done. At present, the church is not how He totally instructed it to be according to the word of God. Some of the churches are practicing "traditions of men." God is not the author of confusion and His Church will be made perfect in His image and in His likeness. ***"So God created man in His own image, in the image of God created he him;" Genesis 1:27a (KJV).*** We are the church therefore, when we as the body of Christ turn our hearts to God and release our ***'will'*** back to Him, that's when we will become pliable for the master's use. I will continue to hold the scripture in my spirit, ***"…nevertheless not my will, but thine, be done." (Luke 22:42b KJV).***

Urgent Update!

I'd like to share with you my very last event that occurred in North Carolina when I visited my friend Kathy. I met Kathy in 2014 on a missionary trip to S. Africa. After that trip, Kathy and I remained close. We talked at least every other week. She shared with me concerning the prophetic movement that was occurring at her church. During one phone conversation Kathy invited me to visit her home in North Carolina. I felt led of the Lord to seek an appointment for prayer with her pastor. I asked my friend to ask her pastor if I could get an appointment for prayer with him. And, his response was, yes. I'd finished my last assignment that God had told me to do. This is the word of the Lord that was given to me on January 9th, 2020 through Pastor Purcell: I felt a need to add this to my story even though I was finished with it (at least that's what I thought).

Pastor Purcell shared, "God has called you into prophetic intercession and you are to take your place. God will teach your hands to war and how to pray by His Spirit. God wants to reveal His mind to you so that you can pray and to also put on your armor which is a mindset. It's all about moving forward. God's going to teach and give you His heart to intercede. You are to pray one hour daily, and God will speak. God's going to take you in a different direction. It's about His will not yours. God has called you as a watchman: He wants to reveal some things that are coming to you through dreams and visions. Therefore, be alert and tuned into Him**."**

Pastor Purcell declared a prayer over me to receive. He said, "This very day Lord, I declare before the seen and unseen that Jesus is your husband. He's head over your household. Lord may the heavens be open, and may your kingdom come, and your will be done. I exercise my will as your ***'wife'*** to give my heart to you. Come, take over. May the angels come over this house and your blood be upon our home. Hence forth, lets do business! Anything else that's contrary to that, I exercise my will in Jesus name, you're not welcome in this home, go! In the name of Jesus! I plead the blood over my life and our home. Lord, I thank you that you're keeping our home safe as a protector. My life's in your hands, in Jesus name!"

"God will cause you to recover all if you do as you're instructed by Him. Change is here! Therefore, you must change the way you do things. God will NOT put new wine in an old wine skin. These things must change. This is a complete shift from where you were during your marriage. You will also have a new mind set and a new makeover."

The very last thing Pastor Purcell shared:
Pastor Purcell was led of the Lord to give me a prayer shawl. He prayed over me and anointed my head with oil. Pastor Purcell had anointed me as a prayer warrior, and he instructed me to wear the prayer shawl each time I prayed. I'm to make sure a chair is right next to me or whichever way I pray to make room for God's presence. Because God would be sitting right next to me. This will be my personal time with Jesus' and it won't be about me. Also, I must let God know I'm available for the next assignment. That's it! Its all about Him first and foremost!

I had gotten sidetracked by focusing on what the enemy was doing instead of keeping my eyes on the one that saves, delivers, and sets free. John 8:38 says, ***"So, if the Son sets you free, you will be free indeed."*** Now, God has my undivided attention fully no matter what may come or go. My assignment is to do my Father's will. This information is vital to me and I felt a need to share this because it's the closing part of my story. Why? Because it's the beginning of the rest of my life!

Contact: <u>asher.cloud@icloud.com</u>

For more copies go to: Amazon.com

www.ingramcontent.com/pod-product-compliance
Lightning Source LLC
Chambersburg PA
CBHW051003050726
47592CB00007B/2683